Habitats

SWAMPLAND

BY
BRIAN E. ABLEMAN

 **Children's Press**

A Division of Grolier Publishing
New York London Hong Kong Sydney
Danbury, Connecticut

Created and Developed by The Learning Source

Designed by Josh Simons

All illustrations by Glenn Quist

Photo Credits: David M. Dennis/ Tom Stack
& Associates: 10 (right bottom); Richard B.
Dippold/Unicorn Stock Photos: 27; Kerry T.
Givens/Tom Stack: 7; Jeff
Greenberg/Unicorn: 20-21; Bernard
Hehl/Unicorn: 1; Judy Hile/Unicorn: 11;
Tom & Pat Leeson: 28 (left); Joe
McDonald/Tom Stack: 10 (right top), 12, 13
(left), 18; Margo Moss/Unicorn: 8 (left), 28
(right), back cover; Brian Parker/Tom Stack:
19; Fred Reischl/Unicorn: 4-5, 15 (top), 17;
John Shaw/Tom Stack: front cover; Tom
Stack/Tom Stack: 9, 29; SuperStock, Inc.:
10 (left), 23; Lynn M. Stone: 2, 6, 8 (right),
13 (right), 14, 15 (bottom), 22, 25, 26, 32.

Library of Congress Cataloging-in-Publication Data
Ableman, Brian E.
      Swampland / by Brian E. Ableman.
         p.   cm. — (Habitats)
      Summary: Describes the characteristics of the Okefenokee Swamp and the animals that live
there.
      ISBN 0-516-20743-1 (lib. bdg.)   0-516-20374-6 (pbk.)
      1. Swamp animals—Okefenokee Swamp (Ga. and Fla.)—Juvenile literature. 2. Swamp
ecology—Okefenokee Swamp (Ga. and Fla.)—Juvenile literature. [1. Swamp animals. 2. Swamp
ecology. 3. Ecology. 4. Okefenokee Swamp (Ga. and Fla.)] I. Title. II. Series: Habitats (Children's
Press)
QL 114.A25   1997
591.768'09758'752—dc21   97-26986   CIP
                                                                   AC

Printed in Mexico
        7 8 9 10 R 06

Tucked away in the southeastern corner of the United States, nearly forgotten, lies an ancient, watery world called Okefenokee (oh kee fen OH kee). It is a swamp, a squishy place where the air and land are almost as dark and wet as the water.

It is dawn now in the Okefenokee, but only a stray sunbeam or two ever reach the ground. A thick overgrowth of trees, shrubs, and bushes screens out most of the light.

mosquito

As the sun comes up, the air buzzes with the sound of insect wings. Gnats so small that they are almost invisible swarm in the trees. Katydids feed on tender leaves while dragonflies grow fat as they gobble up mosquito after mosquito.

In this soggy place the plants, too, can be fierce. A spider stops to rest on a leaf. It snoops around the plant until, in a flash, it topples down a tube and disappears forever. The spider has become a tasty meal for the insect-eating pitcher plant.

Cypress trees like these stretch 120 feet (36.6 meters) up into the sky. As they struggle to reach their own patch of sunlight, the trees twist into strange shapes that look like knees and legs and arms.

In spite of its name, Spanish moss is not really moss at all. It actually is an organism called an epiphyte (EP ah fight). Spanish moss gets its food from the air and rainwater. Scaly hairs on the stems give the plant its gray color.

Hanging from the limbs of cypress trees are long, hairy clumps of Spanish moss. In the flickering light, the moss-covered trees seem to turn into spooky ghosts and goblins.

Frogs are everywhere. So are salamanders. They hop, scurry, and hide, doing whatever they can to escape all the hungry predators around them.

A giant snapping turtle has a wiggly growth on its tongue. The turtle shakes this growth from side to side. Passing fish sometimes mistake it for a swimming worm and end up as the turtle's dinner.

Turtles roam the land and the water. Small ones use their shells as protection from enemies. But giant snapping turtles, which can weigh as much as 150 pounds (67.5 kilograms), have little to fear.

Many kinds of snakes slither through the water,
trees, and grass. Some, like this water snake, can only
do harm to creatures smaller or slower than they are.

Other snakes, such as this poisonous cottonmouth, are dangerous to almost everything. A cottonmouth will swim or hang almost unseen from a tree limb. Then, without warning, it will attack some unsuspecting animal.

The absolute ruler of the swamp is the mighty alligator. As an adult, it often grows to 15 feet (4.6 meters) of muscle, scaly hide, and big teeth. An alligator will eat almost anything, even another alligator.

When the weather grows cool, an alligator's digestive system slows down almost to a stop. This leaves the alligator feeling so full that even turtles can sit safely nearby.

By day, an alligator usually rests, sunning itself or floating, like a log, in the water. But by night the alligator hunts, feasting on frogs, turtles, or even birds and small mammals.

A female alligator makes a nest by piling up plants and roots. Then she wiggles her body on the pile to make a deep hole for her eggs. There the eggs can stay, safe and warm, until they are ready to hatch.

After they leave their shells, baby alligators are closely watched by their mother. Slowly, the youngsters learn the ways of the swamp. In time they will be off on their own.

If the eggs in an alligator nest become too cool, only females will hatch. Only males will hatch if the eggs are too warm. To make an even balance of males and females, the mother alligator uses her body to control the temperature in the nest.

Otters and other mammals hunt or fish in the swamp.
But they are always on guard, alert to the dangers
around them.
   In most habitats on earth, mammals usually rule. In the
swamp, however, reptiles seem to have the upper hand.

Yet, the mammals continue to come. Raccoons seek places to hunt. Opossums, such as this one, find homes wherever they can.

Close by, in the shallow waters of the swamp, a pine-covered island rises. Here, some larger mammals can sometimes find a comfortable home. This little fawn, for instance, lives well, nibbling on the island's plentiful supply of shrubs and trees.

Bobcats, too, roam among the pines. Fast and deadly predators, these fierce wildcats hunt whatever they please. Young deer and wild pigs must be especially careful to stay out of their way.

At one time, magnificent Florida panthers were common in the swamp. Now it is rare to see one on the island or anywhere else in the Okefenokee.

The largest mammals in the swamp are black bears. Like this fellow, they are often seen lumbering through bushes or clambering up trees in search of tasty bugs.

The voice of the swamp definitely belongs to the birds and insects. Any time of day, an orchestra of cheeps, caws, and buzzes can be heard. Small birds, such as mocking birds and redwing blackbirds, live in shrubs and trees. Here, it is very easy to find noisy insects and juicy berries to eat.

Large sandhill cranes wade into the shallow swamp water, looking for food. They poke around, using their long beaks to catch tasty fish that swim by.

This bird's bill is like a great shovel. Standing in shallow water, it moves its bill back and forth. When the bill touches something, it snaps shut, trapping the bird's meal inside.

Here, too, the roseate spoonbill makes its home. Fifty years ago this red-feathered bird was nearly extinct. Now, there are more than 1,000 nesting pairs alive.

Nearby, an anhinga swims at top speed to trap and eat a frog. Then the water-soaked bird comes ashore to dry out. Unlike most birds, anhingas do not have a waxy coating on their wings. So instead of sliding off, water soaks through the birds' feathers, leaving it no choice but to hang out to dry.

As night falls, herons return home with food for their hungry chicks. Most of the birds will sleep now.

But for some mammals, insects, and reptiles night is the time to hunt. After floating all day in the water, this alligator is looking for a big meal.

The setting sun brings with it the buzzing of insects and the squishing and splashing of hungry animals on the prowl. Here in the swamp, life continues as it has for thousands of years, untouched, except for the water, the weather, and the creatures that call it home.

More About

Anhinga, Page 1:
The anhinga is also known as a "darter." The name comes from the way these birds use their long necks and sharp-pointed bills to spear, or dart, fish.

Frogs, Page 10:
Most frogs actually can jump as much as 20 times their own body lengths. Measure out 20 times your body length and see if you can jump that far!

The Everglades, Pages 4-5:
The Everglades is a swamp more than four times the size of the Okefenokee. It covers more than 2,746 square miles (7,112 square kilometers) of southern Florida.

Salamander, Page 10:
If a salamander gets a leg or tail caught or bitten off, it has nothing to worry about. Salamanders have the amazing ability to grow new limbs to replace ones that are lost!

Spider, Page 7:
A spider's web is so strong that even insects much bigger and stronger than spiders cannot escape from it.

Snapping Turtle, Page 11:
Most turtles have large shells to protect them from enemies. But not the snapping turtle. Its shell is so small that it depends on its strong jaws for defense.

This Habitat

Snake, Page 12:

Snakes use their teeth for capturing prey, not eating it. They open their big, stretchable jaws and swallow their prey whole—while it is still alive.

Opossum, Page 19:

Opossums are related to kangaroos and other animals that carry their young in pouches. Opossums also have 50 teeth, more than any other mammal in North America!

Alligator, Page 14:

Alligators and crocodiles are related and can be difficult to tell apart. But crocodiles have a more pointed snout. They also weigh less and grow more quickly.

Florida Panther, Page 22:

This rare animal actually is a mountain lion. It is such an excellent jumper that it often pounces on its prey from high up on the limb of a tree.

Otter, Page 18:

Otters are such expert swimmers that they can stay under water for up to four minutes at a time. They even have ears and nostrils that close in order to keep out water.

Sandhill Crane, Page 25:

Nearly five feet (1.52 meters) tall, sandhill cranes are able to see over the tall grasses and bushes of the swamp. Their loud cry, like a bugle call, warns creatures of coming danger.